EAGLES

Written and edited by **Lucy Baker**

Consultant Ian Dawson, Librarian,
Royal Society for the Protection of Birds

TWO-CAN

First published in Great Britain in 1990 by
Two-Can Publishing Ltd
27 Cowper Street
London EC2A 4AP

© Two-Can Publishing Ltd, 1990

© Text Lucy Baker, 1990
Artworked by Sarah Dobinson
Printed in Portugal

British Library Cataloguing in Publication Data

Baker, Lucy
Eagles
1. Eagles
I. Title
598.9'16

ISBN 1-85434-076-x

Photograhic Credits:
Front cover Frank Lane p.4 Jeff Foott/Bruce Coleman p.5 Stephen J. Krasemann/Bruce Coleman p.6-7 G. W. Elison/Frank Lane p.8 Leonard Lee Rue III/Bruce Coleman p.9
left M Newman/Frank Lane right Peter Johnson/NHPA p.10 Peter Johnson/NHPA p.11 Leonard Lee Rue III/Bruce Coleman p.13 J. L. G. Grande/Bruce Coleman p.14
J. L. G. Grande/Bruce Coleman p.15 top Dieter & Mary Plage/Bruce Coleman bottom Clem Haagner/Ardea p.16 J. Swedberg/Ardea p.17 Leonard Lee Rue III/Bruce
Coleman p.18 Lacz Lemoine/NHPA p.19 Bruce Coleman

Illustration Credits:
p.4-21 David Cook/Linden Artists p.24-25 Malcolm Livingstone p.26-30 Stephen Lings/Linden Artists p.31 Alan Rogers

CONTENTS

LOOKING AT EAGLES

Eagles are fierce looking birds with hooked beaks and needle-sharp claws. They are famed for their soaring flight and excellent hunting skills. Eagles have been used as symbols of strength and freedom around the world. The bald eagle is the national symbol of the USA.

Eagles belong to a large group of birds that includes buzzards, falcons, hawks, kites and vultures. They are birds of prey which means they hunt and eat meat.

Eagles are heavily-built birds with large wings and strong legs. Their eyes can be blue, brown or a piercing yellow colour. Most eagles' feathers are brown or black with patches of white.

▲ The yellow feet and sharp claws of the bald eagle. Eagles' claws are called talons and they are used to grasp and kill the birds' prey.

▶ There are about 60 different types of eagles in the world, including the bald eagle. Bald eagles are found in North America. Mature bald eagles are easily recognised by their white head feathers and yellow beaks. Young bald eagles have a speckled brown plumage and dark beaks.

EAGLE FACTS

The largest eagles measure up to two metres (over seven feet) from wing tip to wing tip.

The eagle's clawed feet can be as large as a man's hands.

HIGH FLIERS

You are more likely to see an eagle in the sky than on the ground. The bird's long, broad wings and tail make it clumsy on land, but in the air it travels with speed and grace. Large eagles can fly over 320 kilometres (200 miles) every day. The eagle's soaring flight has earned it a reputation as the king of all birds.

Eagles soar by using the wind, like kites. Wind blowing across the land flows upwards over hills, mountains

and other obstacles. Eagles catch the wind as it rises and ride it. They also catch currents of air called heat thermals that rise from the ground as it warms up each day. With little effort, eagles can be carried up 2000 metres (6500 feet) by heat thermals.

When eagles soar, they hold their long wings out straight or in a shallow 'v'. At the tips of the eagles' wings, the feathers are spread out like fingers. By moving different parts of their wings and tails, eagles control their soaring flight and travel great distances with little effort.

THE EAGLE'S HOME

Eagles can be seen flying in wild, remote places around the world. Some eagles live on mountains or open grasslands, others live near the coast or in dense woodlands. Many eagles choose to live alone, but a few, like the bald eagles, live in small groups.

The eagle's home is an area of land called its territory. This may be no bigger than a football stadium, but large birds, like the golden eagle, can rule up to 400 square kilometres (250 square miles) of open countryside.

Most eagles stay in their home territory all year round, but a few travel south each winter or move on when food becomes difficult to find.

▼ Golden eagles are aggressive birds that live alone. They can be found in countries around the world, living on mountains and rugged lands.

▲ Eagles drink from small pools of water, lakes and streams. They may also wash in the water. The bateleur eagle, above, is one of several snake eagles. It lives in southern parts of Africa.

◀ Bald eagles are sociable birds and can often be seen feeding or roosting together. They belong to a group of eagles called fish or sea eagles that live near coastlines.

Eagles mark out their territory with breathtaking aerial displays and loud, squawking calls. When other birds of prey stray onto their land, they are challenged or attacked.

Eagles defend their territory most actively during the mating season and while they are raising their young. Eagles begin mating when they are about five years old. Individual birds perform daring flying stunts to win and keep their mates. Sometimes courting couples join talons and cartwheel together in mid-flight.

NESTS IN THE SKY

Eagle couples build their nests in treetops or high up on a cliff ledge. The nests are called eyries. Most eagles use their eyries over and over again and each mating season they add more twigs to them. Over the years old eyries can become huge structures. They are used until they are blown down in a storm or the tree they are built on collapses.

Eagles may spend several weeks preparing their nest site before mating. As a final touch, they often add a soft layer of fresh, leafy twigs to the top of the nest.

After mating, the female eagle lays one to three eggs. The eggs are usually pale green at first, but turn white after a few days. The eggs have to be kept warm and safe until they hatch, so one of the parents sits on the nest while the other defends the territory and finds food. Sometimes the mother bird stays on the nest all the time, but often both birds take turns.

◀ A black eagle prepares to land at its nest site, situated high up on a cliff ledge.

▼ Can you see the eagle's giant nest hidden in the pine trees below?

NESTING FACTS

The largest nest in the world was built by bald eagles. It weighed as much as two cars and took over 35 years to make.

Not all eagles build huge nests. Snake eagles make small, flimsy nests each time they mate.

FROM EGG TO EAGLE

Baby eagles, called eaglets, are weak and helpless when they hatch from their shells. At first, they do little more than shuffle around their nests. Eaglets eat small pieces of meat offered to them by their parents in the first week or so. Then as they get stronger, they are given whole prey to tear up.

It can take up to four months for eaglets to develop their flight feathers. During this time, they must be fed several times daily and sheltered from rain, hot sunshine and predators.

Once the young birds have all their feathers, they have to master flying and hunting skills. To help them learn, their parents play games that test their reactions, like dropping food to them while they are flying.

Some eagle families stay together for over a year while their young learn how to survive. The training is difficult and only one in four eaglets survives its first year of life. Eaglets that do make it to adulthood can live for 30 years.

▶ Fights among growing eaglets are common and it is rare for more than one eaglet to survive in the nest. However, these two Spanish imperial eaglets seem happy to grow up side by side.

EAGLET FACTS

Eaglets are covered in silky down at first. Their bleary eyes are open, but they cannot lift their heads or move around.

10-42 days
Wing and tail feathers appear, giving eaglets a scruffy appearance.

7-21 days
Eaglets' silky down is replaced by a thicker coat and they are more active.

42-120 days
Eaglets are almost fully grown. They practice wing flapping before taking their first flight.

HUNT TO KILL

Eagles hunt by day. Perched in treetops or sailing across the sky, they scan the ground in search of their next meal. When they see suitable prey, they swoop down and strike.

Eagles are well suited to a hunting life. Their flying skills are unmatched. Their keen eyesight, which is believed to be at least twice as sharp as ours, allows them to pick out small prey from a distance. And their powerful, clawed feet grasp and kill in seconds.

Eagles eat many different kinds of meat. Mice, voles, rabbits and similar animals form the basic diet of many eagles, but birds, reptiles and insects may be eaten. The biggest eagles hunt small antelopes, monkeys and sloths.

Sea and fish eagles are expert fishermen, and other eagles catch fish as part of their diet. Eagles prefer to catch fish at the surface of the water, but a few will plunge in until almost submerged. Bald eagles swim to shore when they get too wet to fly. Some sea eagles also hunt sea snakes, scooping them out of the water as they surface to breathe.

◄ Snake eagles, like the short-toed eagle shown here, have smaller feet than other eagles. This helps them keep hold of their slippery prey. Snake eagles do not just eat snakes. Lizards, frogs and small mammals form part of their diet.

Most snake eagles live in warm, tropical parts of the world where snakes and lizards can be found throughout the year. Snake eagles that live in cooler climates fly south each winter when their usual prey become too difficult to find.

▲ This white-bellied sea eagle has seen its prey. Throwing its wings back and its feet forward, it is about to impale a fish on its sharp talons.

► Having plucked a buzzard from the sky, this martial eagle is eating its meal cautiously. Martial eagles hunt over wooded lands in southern parts of Africa.

Sometimes eagles kill their prey by grip alone. Otherwise they may stab their sharp talons into the head or neck of their victim. If their prey is too large to be swallowed whole, eagles tear it apart with their strong, hooked beaks. Big kills may even be cut into pieces and hidden in the eagles' hunting grounds.

SCAVENGERS AND PIRATES

Apart from catching and eating their own food, many eagles eat carrion like their cousins the vultures. Carrion is the rotting flesh of animals that have died from natural causes or have been killed by other animals. Birds that eat carrion are called scavengers.

Some eagles only eat carrion in the winter when their usual prey becomes too difficult to find. Others, like the bateleur eagles, scavenge all year round.

Some eagles are also pirates, stealing food from other meat-eating birds rather than catching their own. Often, the food is stolen in spectacular mid-flight attacks. Bateleur eagles, tawny eagles and several fish and sea eagles are pirates.

▼ Immature bald eagles battle for feasting rights on a piece of carrion. Arguments between eagles are usually decided quickly, as neither bird can afford to damage its flight feathers.

▲ This golden eagle is covering its food with its wings while eating. This is a protective gesture called mantling. Eagles have to protect their kill from other predators, especially other birds of prey. Mantling is one way of doing this. Other tactics include loud, aggressive calls, and threatening poses.

FEEDING FACTS

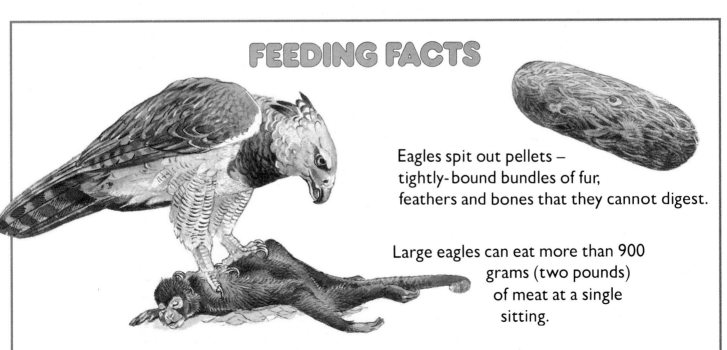

Eagles spit out pellets – tightly-bound bundles of fur, feathers and bones that they cannot digest.

Large eagles can eat more than 900 grams (two pounds) of meat at a single sitting.

EAGLES AND PEOPLE

Today, many eagles face problems that are caused by people. The greatest problem is loss of habitat. Some eagles hunt over large tracts of wild land. If these areas are changed or developed, eagles find it difficult to find enough food to survive.

The Madagascar serpent eagle and the monkey-eating eagle of the Philippines are probably the world's most threatened eagles. Both birds live in rainforests that are rapidly disappearing.

Another danger that a lot of eagles face is the hunter with his gun. Some people shoot eagles for sport, and farmers will fire at them if they approach their sheep, pheasants or other livestock.

Wildlife groups around the world are trying to help eagles. In some countries special areas of land are preserved so that the birds can live in peace. Climbers and walkers can also upset eagles, so if you see an eagle try not to disturb it.

► The monkey-eating eagle is threatened because its rainforest home is rapidly disappearing. These magnificent birds have also been hunted by locals to be stuffed and sold as ornaments to tourists.

▲ Falconers wear thick, leather gloves when they handle their birds. This captive bird is an imperial eagle.

FALCONRY

In some parts of the world, people keep eagles and train them to kill wolves, foxes and similar prey. This is called falconry. Falconry birds are hooded when they go out hunting. They have their masks removed when their prey are in sight.

MOUNTAIN GAME

Follow the eagles as they prepare for their nesting season. To play this game you will need a dice and some counters.

BE CAREFUL – if you land on a black square you have to start again.

START

Find a mate. Throw again.

Stop to drink. Miss a turn.

Storm blows you off course. Back 4 spaces.

Chase rabbit, but it gets away. Miss a turn.

Gather twigs for nest. Forward 3 spaces.

Attack intruder.
Miss a turn.

Wings clipped.
Rest for a turn.

Successful hunt.
Forward 4 spaces.

Strong winds.
Soar forward
4 spaces.

Stop for mutual
preening.
Miss a turn.

Catch a hare
and hurry home.
Forward 3 spaces.

FINISH

EAGLE MASK

There are lots of ways to decorate masks. Here are a few things to try.

wool

string

straws

crayons

brown

white

red

paint

fabric

coloured paper

▶ Our mask was made by cutting out this basic shape from card and covering it with paper.

Try making a mask. It's easy to do and fun to wear. All you need is a piece of card or thick paper, a length of elastic, string or lace and a pair of scissors.

Draw a basic mask shape on to the card. Remember to make two holes for your eyes and a small hole at each side of the mask. Carefully cut out your mask shape and then decide how you are going to decorate it. Try some of the ideas in the picture on the left. When your mask is decorated, thread the elastic, string or lace through the two holes at the side of the mask. Now your mask is ready to wear!

FIND THE EAGLES

There are six eagles hiding in this picture. Can you find them all?

There is one more animal in the picture. Do you know its name?

KING OF THE SKIES

BY LUCY BAKER

One day Arthur the young eaglet would be a master of the sky; a king among birds. Now, lying helplessly in his nest, he did not look like a royal bird. He could not stand or beat his wings. He could not even lift his head.

Arthur had just struggled out of his eggshell. It had taken him over 20 hours to hatch and he was very tired. From under half-closed eyelids, he saw his mother standing over him and, beyond the sticks and leaves of the nest, a brilliant blue sky. His lids dropped and Arthur fell asleep.

The next morning Arthur woke to find his mother beside him. She had a ribbon of meat hanging from her beak. With great effort, Arthur

stretched up, snatched the tiny morsel and swallowed it in one gulp. His mother had more food to give him but by the time she had picked it up, Arthur had fallen back to sleep.

Eating and sleeping took up most of Arthur's time at first, but with each meal that he ate, his strength grew.

While Arthur was very young he was never left alone. One of his

parents was always close by to shelter him from the sun or feed him small pieces of meat. Then, as he grew, they began to leave him for hours at a time

and, instead of feeding him bit by bit, they dropped whole prey that he had to tear apart himself.

Whenever Arthur was alone, he scrambled to the edge of his eyrie and watched the world around him. It was a spectacular world of towering mountains and wide, empty valleys. There was even a clear blue lake glistening in the distance.

From the cliff edge, Arthur studied his parents' graceful flight. He held out his scruffy, undeveloped wings and imagined that he, too, was soaring across the sky. He longed for a time when he could leave the nest and explore his parents' kingdom.

Then, at last, Arthur's moment came. One morning he woke more restless than ever. He had all his feathers now and it was time to fly.

Poised on the edge of his nest, Arthur pushed off with his powerful feet and launched himself into the sky. He was airborne! Arthur screamed in delight as he soared along. Then he tried moving his wings and tail to make himself twist and turn, rise and fall.

Arthur's parents saw him flying and circled near him to show their

approval. Now he was beginning to look like a royal bird.

After his first flight, nothing could keep Arthur out of the sky. Every morning he left the eyrie to practise what he had learned. He wheeled and glided, flapped and circled, soared and dived. He looked strong and majestic.

Arthur's parents were proud of his flying skills, but they still had to hunt food for him to eat. Until he learned to hunt for himself, he would be a prince, not a king.

A month after Arthur had taken to the air, he had still not made a kill. His parents were beginning to worry – without hunting skills how would he survive? Then one day things changed.

Arthur was out showing off his soaring skills when he spotted a movement on the ground. His needle-sharp eyes focused on a small rabbit scampering through the grass below.

In a split second, he measured distance, speed and direction. He made a breathtaking dive. Seconds later he rose again, with the rabbit hanging helplessly in his talons.

Arthur soared high in the sky with his kill and called out to his parents. He had made it. He was no longer an eaglet or a prince, now he was a king. He would not leave his parents' kingdom for a while, but when he did, he would be able to survive.

TRUE OR FALSE ?

Which of these facts are true and which ones are false? If you have read this book carefully, you will know the answers.

1. The golden eagle is the national symbol of the USA.

2. Eagles are birds of prey.
3. Eagles eat nuts, seeds and berries.
4. The eagle is sometimes called the king of all birds.

5. The eagle's home is an area of land called its territory.
6. Eagles live in large flocks.
7. Courting eagles may join talons and cartwheel together in mid-flight.

8. Eagles' nests are called eyries.
9. The smallest nest in the world was built by eagles.

10. Only one in four eaglets makes it to adult life.
11. Eagles have poor eyesight.

12. Eagles can fly over 320 kilometres (200 miles) in a day.
13. Eagles catch their prey with their hooked beaks.
14. Baby eagles are called eaglets.
15. Some people train eagles to kill wolves, foxes and similar prey.